Amer In 50 Events

James Weber

About the Author:

James Weber is an author and journalist. He has a passion for literature and loves writing about social sciences, focusing on history, economics and politics. His hobbies include rowing, hiking and any other outdoor activity. James is married and has two kids.

Other Books in the *History in 50 Events* Series

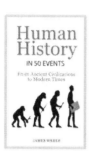
Human History
IN 50 EVENTS
From Ancient Civilizations to Modern Times
JAMES WEBER

Ancient History
IN 50 EVENTS
From the First Civilizations to the Fall of the Roman Empire
JAMES WEBER

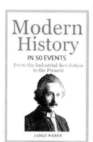
Modern History
IN 50 EVENTS
From the Industrial Revolution to the Present
JAMES WEBER

World History
IN 50 EVENTS
From the Beginning of Time to the Present
JAMES WEBER

American History
IN 50 EVENTS
From Early Immigration to World Power
JAMES WEBER

WORLD WAR II
IN 50 EVENTS
From the Very Beginning to the Fall of the Axis Powers
JAMES WEBER

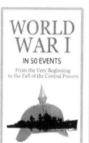
WORLD WAR I
IN 50 EVENTS
From the Very Beginning to the Fall of the Central Powers
JAMES WEBER

VIETNAM WAR
IN 50 EVENTS
From the First Indochina War to the Fall of Saigon
JAMES WEBER

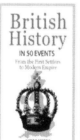
British History
IN 50 EVENTS
From the First Settlers to Modern Empire
JAMES WEBER

The 20th Century
IN 50 EVENTS
The Most Important Inventions, Conflicts, Technologies & Much More
JAMES WEBER

Christian History
IN 50 EVENTS
From the Old Testament to Modern Times
JAMES WEBER

Content

Introduction

The United States is a fascinating country. Founded by immigrants looking for a better life, it became the leading world power in less than 200 years. Today, the USA stands for Life, Liberty, and the Pursuit of Happiness. You will see that these values were not chosen at random, but were the answer to oppressive colonialism and limited freedom in the "old world." I myself was motivated to write this book by a question every student of American history asks himself:

How did the United States of America become the country it is today?

Change and innovation happen every day, but they are more easily understood if we look at single events that symbolize something new. The 50 events in this book are meant to give you a quick but comprehensive summary of an entire country's history. This limited space forced me to leave out events that others might have included. While I tried to be as scientific as possible, there will always be a debate over the importance of some events over others, but do not worry – I made sure to include all the major turning points, such as the Declaration of Independence, the Great Depression, and World War II. I hope you enjoy this book just as much as I enjoyed writing it.

-   James Weber

James Weber

The Beginning: From the First Indians to the Declaration of Independence

14,500 B.C. - The First Indians Settle on the American Continent

The American continent was first settled by people from Asia who migrated slowly across the Bering land bridge, which connected Asia with North America and was roughly 1,000 miles (1,600 km) wide. Even though there are many theories about the origin of these first migrations, it is still unclear when and how many of these first settlers came. Due to archeological evidence, it is probable that the Paleo-Indians' first "widespread" habitation of the Americas occurred during the final years of the last glacial period or, more specifically, what historians call the late glacial maximum, around 16,500–13,000 years ago.

Graphic of the migrations in and out of the Americas, illustrated by the gene flow.

After reaching Alaska, they migrated into northern Canada, south along the Pacific Coast, into the interior of Canada, and south to the Great Plains and the American Southwest. They were the earliest ancestors of the "Athabascan-speaking peoples," which include the present-day and historical Navajo and Apache.

2) 1,000 A.D. - Leif Erikson is the First European to Land in North America

Nearly 500 years before Christopher Columbus, the Nordic explorer Leif Erikson reached North America and, according to the Sagas of Icelanders, established a settlement at Vinland, the northern tip of Newfoundland in modern-day Canada. Likely to have been born in Iceland, Erikson was blown off course when travelling from Norway to Greenland to a shore that he did not expect to see, where "self-sown wheat fields and grapevines" caught his eye. After traveling back to Greenland, he purchased a new ship, gathered a crew of 35 men, and organized an expedition to build a settlement on the newly discovered land.

Leiv Eiriksson Discovers America by Christian Krohg (1893)

After arriving on the Canadian coast, he decided to encamp there for the winter and broke his party into two groups - one to remain at camp and the other to explore the lands. During one of these explorations, they discovered that the land was full of vines and grapes. Leif therefore named the land "Vinland." There, he and his crew built a small settlement, which later visitors from Greenland called Leifsbúðir (Leif's Booths). After having wintered over in Vinland, Leif went back to Greenland in the spring with a cargo of timber and grapes.

3) 1492 - Christopher Columbus Discovers America

In the context of emerging Western imperialism and economic competition between European kingdoms in the 15th century, the establishment of new trade routes and colonies became more important, and the Spanish Crown financed an Italian explorer called Christopher Columbus to reach the East Indies by sailing westward. In 1492, Columbus led three ships across the Atlantic in search of a short route to Asia. They first found land on an island in The Bahamas in Central America. Columbus referred to the native people living there as "Indians," believing he had actually reached "The Indies" in Asia. He continued to believe this until the end of his life.

Christopher Columbus discovers The Americas, painting by John Vanderlyn

Although Columbus was not the first European explorer to reach the Americas, his voyages led to the first lasting European contact with the Americas, inaugurating a period of European exploration, conquest, and colonization that lasted for several centuries. They had, therefore, an enormous impact in the historical development of the modern Western world. Columbus himself saw his accomplishments primarily in the light of spreading the Christian religion.

4) 1497 - John Cabot Claims North America for England

John Cabot was an Italian-born English explorer and navigator whose original name was Giovanni Caboto. After Columbus had claimed the southern half of the New World for Spain, the English King Henry VII requested Cabot to sail to what is now Canada in order to secure land for the English Empire. Cabot landed near

Labrador, Newfoundland, or Cape Breton Island (the exact spot is uncertain) on June 24, 1497. He explored the Canadian coastline and named many of its islands and capes. Part of the mission was to search for a northwest passage across North America to Asia, in which Cabot was unsuccessful, although he thought that he had reached northeastern Asia.

Cabot Statue in Bristol, England

Shortly after returning to England, Cabot set sail for his second voyage, during which he mysteriously disappeared. Rumors that the Spanish murdered him spread quickly, and soon, England and Spain struggled to carve out their own areas of interest in the mainland and on the islands of the Americas.

5) 1565 - Saint Augustine Becomes the First Permanent European Colony in the United States

St. Augustine is the oldest continuously occupied settlement of European origin in the United States. The settlement was established forty-two years before the English colonized Jamestown and fifty-five years before the Pilgrims landed at Plymouth Rock. Attempts of settlements prior to the founding of St. Augustine were made by both Spain and France, but failed.

City Gate, St. Augustine around 1861

On September 8, 1565, Pedro Menéndez de Avilés landed on the shore of what is now called Matanzas Bay and named the area San Agustin. Later, the settlement would be called St. Augustine, Florida. Built on the site of an ancient Native American village, and near the place where Ponce de Leon, the European discoverer of Florida, landed in 1513 in search of the legendary Fountain of Youth, it has been continually inhabited since its founding. Today, the city has a population of almost 70,000 and is a major tourist attraction.

6) 1565 - Jamestown Becomes the First PermanentEnglish Settlement in the United States

In 1606, a group of English entrepreneurs decided to set sail to the New World in order to establish a permanent colony for the English Crown. The mission's captain was Christopher Newport, an English seaman and privateer. His fleet consisted of three ships named *Susan Constant*, *Discovery*, and *Godspeed*. The trip across the Atlantic Ocean took around five months duration and included a stop in Puerto Rico. On April 26, 1607, the expedition made landfall at a place they named Cape Henry, but soon decided to select a more secure location for their settlement.

The ruins of Jamestown showing the tower of the old Jamestown Church built in 1639.

About three weeks later, the expedition selected a piece of land on a large peninsula, some 40 miles (64 km) inland from the Atlantic Ocean, as a prime location for a fortified settlement. A defensible strategic point due to a curve in the river, the channel was close to the land, thus making it navigable (and allowing for ships to dock near enough land for piers or wharves to be built). Perhaps the best thing about it, from an English point of view, was that it was not inhabited by nearby Virginia Indian tribes, who regarded the site as too poor and remote for agriculture. However, the island was swampy, isolated, offered limited space, and was plagued by mosquitoes and brackish tidal river water unsuitable for drinking.

7) 1620 - Pilgrims Establish the Plymouth Colony in Massachusetts

Founded by a group of Separatists initially known as the Brownist Emigration and Anglicans, who together later came to be known as the Pilgrims, Plymouth Colony was, along with Jamestown, one of the earliest successful colonies to be founded by the English in North America, and the first sizable permanent English settlement in the New England region. Aided by Squanto, a Native American of the Patuxet people, the colony was able to establish a treaty with the tribe leader Chief Massasoit, who helped to ensure the colony's success. Ultimately, the colony was merged with the Massachusetts Bay Colony and other territories in 1691 to form the Province of Massachusetts Bay.

The Landing of the Pilgrims (1877) by Henry A. Bacon

Despite the colony's relatively short history, Plymouth holds a special role in U.S. history. Rather than being businessmen like many of the settlers of Jamestown, a significant proportion of the citizens of Plymouth were fleeing religious persecution and seeking a place to worship as they saw fit. The legal and social systems of the colony became closely tied to their religious beliefs, as well as English customs. Most of the events and people surrounding Plymouth Colony have become part of American folklore, including the monument known as Plymouth Rock and the North American tradition known as Thanksgiving.

8) 1754 - The French and Indian War Begins

The *Battle of Jumonville Glen* in May 1754 set off the French and Indian War, which was later part of the Seven Years' War (which many historians regard as the first true World War). On the American continent, the war was fought between the colonies of British America and New France, with both sides supported by military units from their parent countries of Great Britain and France, as well as Native American allies. At the start of the war, the French North American colonies had a population of roughly 60,000 European settlers, compared to two million in the British North American colonies. The outnumbered French particularly depended on the Indians. Long in conflict, the metropole nations declared war on each other in 1756, escalating the war from a regional affair into an international conflict.

Portrait of George Washington shows him wearing his colonel's uniform of the Virginia Regiment, with which he attacked the French.

The war was fought primarily along the frontiers between New France and the British colonies, from Virginia in the South to Nova Scotia in the North. It began with a dispute over control of the confluence of the Allegheny and Monongahela rivers, called the Forks of the Ohio, and the site of the French Fort Duquesne and present-day Pittsburgh, Pennsylvania. The dispute erupted into violence in the Battle of Jumonville Glen, during which Virginia militiamen under the command of 22-year-old George Washington ambushed a French patrol.

9) 1770 - British Troops Fire Into a Mob at the Boston Massacre

On March 5, 1770, growing tensions between the Americans and the English troops in the colonies led to an incident now known as the Boston massacre, in which British Army soldiers killed five civilians and injured six others. English troops had been stationed in the city since 1768 in order to support and protect crown-appointed colonial officials sent to enforce unpopular Parliamentary legislation. During the evening of March 5, a large mob got together outside of the Custom House after a British soldier named Hugh White hit a boy who insulted his commanding officer.

A 19th century print of the scene

The boy ran away and returned with a large mob of angry people. To help protect Hugh White from the people, more British soldiers came by and drew their guns. As the mob grew larger and larger, the scene became more and more chaotic, with snowballs being thrown at the soldiers. After someone in the crowd yelled "fire," some of the soldiers started firing into the crowd.

10) 1773 - Boston Tea Party

The Boston Tea Party is probably the most famous American act of protest against the British Crown before the Revolutionary War. After the Boston Massacre, many Americans felt more and more suppressed by the British. There was no American representative overseas in the British government; nevertheless, the citizens of the colonies were heavily. As merchants had to sell their goods at a loss due to tariffs, many began purchasing smuggled goods and bringing them into the country.

Engraving of American colonists dressed as Native Americans throwing 342 trunks of the cargo that was on the British tea ships into Boston Harbor.

On December 16, 1773, Samuel Adams and a group of demonstrators, some disguised as American Indians, destroyed an entire shipment of tea sent by the East India Company. As a reaction, the British government implemented even stricter laws regarding trade in the Massachusetts colony, including the Intolerable Acts, which stated that Boston Harbor was closed until the colonists paid back all the tea they lost. Many historians regard the Boston Tea Party as one of the key events that would escalate into the American Revolution.

11) 1775 - Battles of Lexington and Concord Set Off the American Revolution

April 19, 1775, marked the date that would forever change American history. The night before, hundreds of British troops had marched from Boston to nearby Concord in order to seize an arms cache. Paul Revere, a silversmith and patriot, alerted the Colonial militia to the approach of the British forces.

19th-century depiction of the Battle of Lexington

A confrontation on the Lexington town green started the fighting, and soon, the British were hastily retreating under intense fire. The American militia were outnumbered and fell back as the British troops proceeded on to Concord. At the North Bridge in Concord, approximately 500 militiamen fought and defeated three companies of the King's troops. The British troops were soon outnumbered as more and more militiamen arrived at the fight scene, and had to retreat to Boston where the next important Battle, the Siege of Boston, would take place.

12) 1776 - The Declaration of Independence Makes United States a Sovereign Nation

On June 7, 1776, Richard Henry Lee, the Virginia statesman, offered a resolution to the Congress stating: "that these United Colonies are, and of right ought to be, free and independent States..."

Following his words, a committee consisting of Thomas Jefferson, John Adams, Benjamin Franklin, Robert R. Livingston, and Roger Sherman was organized to prepare a draft for what would later be known as the Declaration of Independence. Jefferson did most of the writing and presented his copy to the Congress on June 28, 1776.

Depiction of Franklin, Adams, and Jefferson working on the
Declaration

Independence was actually declared on July 2, 1776, at the
Pennsylvania State House. After several discussions and changes to
the original, the Continental Congress approved Jefferson's proposed
Declaration. Two days later, on July 4, with New York abstaining,
twelve of the thirteen delegations to the Continental Congress
approved and ordered the printing of the Declaration.

James Weber

A New Nation: From the Bill of Rights to the Civil War

13) 1791 - The Bill of Rights is Ratified

The ratification of the first ten amendments to the United States Constitution had a great impact on the later development of this new nation. It limits the power of the federal government and guarantees citizens of the United States certain rights like the freedom of speech or religion. James Madison, who was greatly influenced by the British Magna Carta of 1215, wrote the original amendments.

James Madison, "Father of the Constitution" and first author of the Bill of Rights

He introduced a series of thirty-nine amendments to the constitution in the House of Representatives on June 8, 1789. On September 25, 1789, Congress approved 12 articles of amendment to the Constitution, subsequently submitting them to the states for ratification. Contrary to the original proposal from Madison that the articles be incorporated into the main body of the Constitution, they were recommended as "supplemental" additions to it. On December 15, 1791, Articles 3 – 12 became Amendments 1 - 10 of the Constitution after having been ratified by the required number of states.

14) 1803 - The Louisiana Purchase Nearly Doubles the Size of the US

The Louisiana Purchase was a land purchase made by United States president Thomas Jefferson in 1803. He bought the Louisiana territory from France, which at that time was led by Napoleon Bonaparte, for US $15 million. Originally, the delegates sent to France were allowed to spend up to US $10 million in order to buy New Orleans and, if possible, the west bank of the Mississippi River. Since the French government was in desperate need of money and afraid of losing its North American territories to the British, all of the Louisiana territory was offered to the Americans for US $5 million more.

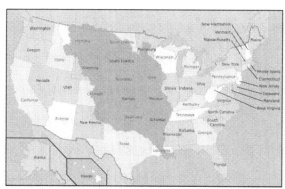

A map of the Louisiana Purchase (green) compared to state boundaries in 2008.

Thomas Jefferson approved the deal and used his constitutional power to sign the necessary treaties. Napoleon Bonaparte had been busy with a war in Europe, and no matter how much he would have liked to invest in the French colonies, his conflicts in Europe had him financially tied up. Jefferson took this as an opportunity to increase the land size of the US, even if it meant going against his republican principles of following the Constitution (which did not grant him the right to buy land).

15) 1804 - Lewis and Clark Begin Their Expedition in St. Louis, Missouri

The Lewis and Clark Expedition was one of the most important expeditions in the US History. On May 14, 1804, two US Army commanders, Meriwether Lewis and William Clark, left St. Charles, Missouri (close to St. Louis) in order to explore the new territory recently bought in the Louisiana Purchase. United States President Thomas Jefferson, who had bought the land from France, chose the two men to lead the expedition. The group included 33 people, mostly Army volunteers.

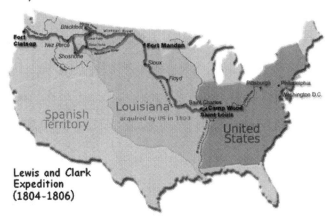

The route of the expedition

They reached the Pacific in 1806, seeing much of what is now the Central and Western United States. Lewis and Clark met their objective of mapping and constituting their presence for a legal claim to the land. They established diplomatic relations and trade with at least two dozen indigenous nations (along the way, the group was joined by a Shoshone Native American woman named Sacagawea, who helped guide them). However, the expedition did not find a continuous waterway to the Pacific Ocean. After their exploration, Lewis became Governor of Louisiana Territory and Clark became Governor of Missouri Territory.

16) 1812 - US Declares War on Britain (War of 1812)

The second direct conflict between the United States and Great Britain after the Revolutionary War is called the War of 1812, and it lasted for almost three years. It followed a time of great stress between the two nations due to the treatment of neutral countries by both France and England during the French Revolutionary and Napoleonic Wars, in which the latter two were antagonists.

Fighting started when the United States attacked the Canadian provinces in 1812, which the British successfully defended. A year later, British and U.S. ships fought in the Battle of Lake Erie, where American forces gained control of the region and invaded and burned Toronto, then called Yorktown.

American commander Oliver Hazard Perry defeats the British at
the Battle of Lake Erie

In 1814, British reinforcements arrived in the United States, who, in
an act of retaliation, burned Washington D.C. and attacked
Baltimore. It was during this battle, that the American lawyer Francis
Scott Key wrote the poem which would later become the national
anthem: "The Star Spangled Banner."

The war's final battle took place in January of 1815, after a
peace treaty had been signed. British troops attacked New
Orleans and lost against American General Andrew Jackson.

17) 1819 - Spain Agrees to Cede Florida to the United States

In the so-called Adams–Onís Treaty of 1819, Spain gave Florida to
the US and defined a new boundary between the US and New Spain
(now Mexico). The treaty settled a standing border dispute between

the two countries and was regarded a triumph of American diplomacy. The negotiations had taken place in the midst of growing tensions related to Spain's territorial boundaries in North America vs. the United States and Great Britain in the aftermath of the American Revolution. Florida had turned into a burden to Spain, who could not afford to send garrisons or settlers.

Map of "East-" and "West Florida"

As a way of saving potential war costs and overseas investments, the Spanish Crown decided to cede the territory to the United States in exchange for settling the boundary dispute in Spanish Texas along the Sabine River. The treaty established the boundary of American claims and territory through the Rocky Mountains and west to the Pacific Ocean. In return, the U.S. paid residents' claims against the Spanish government totaling $5,000,000 and relinquished the U.S. claims on parts of Spanish Texas west of the Sabine River as well as other Spanish areas, under the terms of the Louisiana Purchase.

18) 1820 - Missouri Compromise is Supposed to End Slavery

The Missouri Compromise, also called the Compromise of 1820, was a plan proposed by Henry Clay, a member of House of Representatives, primarily involving the regulation of slavery in the western territories. It admitted Missouri as a slave state to please the South, and Maine as a free state to please the North, thereby keeping the balance of power in the United States Senate between the free states and slave states. The plan also called for slavery to be banned from the Louisiana Territory north of the parallel 36°30☐ north (also known as the Missouri Compromise Line), except within the boundaries of the proposed state of Missouri. It was signed by President James Monroe and passed in 1820.

The Missouri Compromise Line of 1820

Prior to the agreement, the House of Representatives had refused to accept this compromise and a conference committee was appointed. The United States Senate refused to concur in the amendment, and the whole measure was lost.

During the following session, the House passed a similar bill with an amendment, introduced on January 26, 1820, by John W. Taylor of New York, allowing Missouri into the union as a slave state. The question had been complicated by the December admission of Alabama, a slave state, making the number of slave and free states equal.

19) 1823 - Monroe Doctrine Ensures American Independence

On December 2, 1823, President James Monroe declared in a message to Congress that further efforts by European nations to interfere with states in North or South America or colonize land would be interpreted as acts of aggression requiring US intervention. However, the doctrine did accept existing European colonies in the Americas. It was issued at a time when nearly every Latin American colony of Spain and Portugal had achieved or were at the point of gaining independence from the Portuguese and Spanish Empires, therefore having more of a symbolic rather than practical character.

President James Monroe

At the same time, the United States was working in agreement with Britain to ensure that no European power would move in. Regarding the historical context, the doctrine asserted that the Old World and the New World were to remain distinctly separate spheres of influence, for they were composed of entirely separate and independent nations.

20) 1823 - US Further Grows in Size after Mexican–American War

In 1821, when Mexico gained independence from Spain, it allowed non-Spanish settlers to settle in the area. After many years of immigration of European settlers to northern Mexico, disputes led to the Texas Revolution, in which Texas gained its independence from

Mexico. Mexico refused to recognize the new republic as an independent country and threatened war with the United States if it annexed Texas.

Painting of the Battle of Veracruz, a decisive battle in the war

When the US did annex Texas in 1845, Mexico broke off all diplomatic relations. The United States made an offer to buy the land extending from Texas to the Pacific Ocean, which Mexico declined. In 1846, a dispute over the border between Texas and Mexico resulted in armed conflict, which ultimately led to the Mexican–American War, which the United States won after Mexico signed the Treaty of Guadalupe Hidalgo in 1848.

21) 1848 - The California Gold Rush Begins

When James W. Marshall found gold while building a sawmill at Sutter's Mill in Coloma, California, he had no idea what this news would mean for the region. At the time, California was part of the Mexican territory of Alta California, though the US had occupied it in the Mexican-American War.

As the news spread across the United States, more and more people came to California in search of gold or other business opportunities.

Drawing of a man panning for gold

Even though few of them became rich, the effects of the Gold Rush were substantial. San Francisco grew from a small settlement of about 200 residents in 1846 to a boomtown of about 36,000 by 1852. Roads and other towns were built throughout the region. In 1849, a state constitution was written and a governor and legislature were chosen. California became a state as part of the Compromise of 1850. The Gold Rush ended in 1855. At that time, some gold miners went back home, but many stayed and turned California into one of the fastest growing states in the US

22) 1854 - Congress Passes the Kansas-Nebraska Act

The Kansas–Nebraska Act of 1854 created the territories of Kansas and Nebraska, opened these new lands for settlement, and allowed white male settlers in the territories to determine through popular sovereignty whether they wanted to allow slavery within each territory. Democratic Senator Stephen A. Douglas of Illinois designed the act. The initial goal of the Kansas–Nebraska Act was to open up many thousands of new farms and make feasible a Midwestern Transcontinental Railroad.

An early map of the Nebraska and Kansas Territories

33

Douglas believed that the formula of popular sovereignty would ease national tensions over the issue of human bondage and that he would not have to choose a side in the discussion. However, a movement of indignation erupted across the North as anti-slavery elements cried betrayal, due to the fact that Kansas had been officially closed to slavery following the Missouri Compromise of 1820 (which was now repealed).

23) 1861 - The Civil War Begins

1861 marked an important year in American history. On March 4, Abraham Lincoln became president, which led to seven Southern states declaring their independence from the Union and forming the Confederacy, which was supposed to be its own nation, separate and independent from the United States, with Jefferson Davis as their elected president. The U.S government and the states that remained loyal to it did not intend to fight a civil war, as Lincoln stated in his inaugural address.

Union soldiers preparing for battle

34

Fighting began on April 12, 1861, when Confederate forces fired upon Fort Sumter, a key fort held by Union troops in South Carolina. The Union called for every state to provide troops to retake the fort; consequently, four more slave states joined the Confederacy, bringing their total to eleven. Lincoln soon controlled the border states and established a naval blockade that crippled the Southern economy. After four years of fighting, the Confederate states surrendered to the Union after heavy losses in the summer of 1865.

James Weber

Separate but Equal: From Plessy vs. Ferguson to the Great Depression

24) 1863 - Homestead Acts Allow Farmers to Acquire Land Cheaply

The Homestead Acts were several United States federal laws that gave an applicant ownership of land, at little or no cost. In the United States, this originally consisted of grants totaling 160 acres (65 hectares, or one-quarter section) of unappropriated federal land within the boundaries of the public land states. President Abraham Lincoln signed the first of the acts, the Homestead Act of 1862, into law on May 20, 1862. Anyone who had never taken up arms against the US government (including freed slaves and women), was 21 years or older, or was the head of a family could file an application to claim a federal land grant.

Settlers in North Dakota in front of their homestead

A homesteader had to be the head of the household or at least twenty-one years old. They had to live on the designated land, build a home, make improvements, and farm it for a minimum of five years.

Immigrants, farmers without their own land, single women, and former slaves could all qualify. The fundamental racial qualification was that one had to be a citizen, or have filed a declaration of intention to become a citizen, and so the qualification changed over the years with the varying legal qualifications for citizenship. For immigrants, the fundamental qualification was that they had to be permitted to enter the country. During the 1800s, the bulk of immigrants were from Europe, with immigrants from South Asia and East Asia being largely excluded.

25) 1867 - US Acquires Alaska from Russia

The Alaska Purchase was the United States' acquisition of Alaska from the Russian Empire in 1867 by a treaty ratified by the US Senate. Russia wanted to sell its Alaskan territory, fearing that it might be seized if war broke out with Britain. Russia's primary activities in the territory had been fur trade and missionary work among the Native Alaskans. With the purchase of Alaska, the United States added 586,412 square miles (1,518,800 km^2) of new territory.

The signing of the Alaska Treaty on March 30, 1867.

Reactions to the purchase in the United States were mixed, with some opponents calling it "Seward's Folly," while many others praised the move for weakening both Britain and Russia as rivals to American commercial expansion in the Pacific region. Originally organized as the Department of Alaska, the area was renamed the District of Alaska and the Alaska Territory before becoming the modern state of Alaska upon being admitted to the Union as a state in 1959.

26) 1870 - Fifteenth Amendment Gives Blacks the Right to Vote

The Fifteenth Amendment to the United States Constitution was ratified on February 3, 1870. It prohibits the federal and state governments from denying a citizen the right to vote based on "race, color, or previous condition of servitude."

Drawing depicting African Americans casting ballots

In the final years of the American Civil War and the Reconstruction Era that followed, Congress repeatedly debated the rights of the millions of black former slaves. By 1869, amendments had been passed to abolish slavery and provide citizenship and equal protection under the law, but the election of Ulysses S. Grant to the presidency in 1868 convinced a majority of Republicans that protecting the franchise of black voters was important for the party's future. After rejecting more sweeping versions of a suffrage amendment, Congress proposed a compromise amendment banning franchise restrictions based on race, color, or previous servitude on February 26, 1869. The amendment survived a difficult ratification fight and was adopted on March 30, 1870.

27) 1876 - Battle of the Little Bighorn

The Battle of the Little Bighorn marked one of the bloodiest battles between the native Indians (Lakota, Northern Cheyenne, and Arapaho tribes) and the American Cavalry. The battle, which took place from June 25–26, 1876, near the Little Bighorn River in eastern Montana Territory, became the most prominent action of the Great Sioux War of 1876. It symbolized an overwhelming victory for the Lakota, Northern Cheyenne, and Arapaho, led by several major war leaders, including Chief Gall and Crazy Horse, who were inspired by the visions of Sitting Bull.

Illustration of Lieutenant Colonel Custer on horseback and his US
Army troops making their last charge

The US 7th Cavalry, including the Custer Battalion – a force of more
than 600 men led by George Armstrong Custer – suffered a severe
defeat. Several of the 7th Cavalry's twelve companies were
annihilated; Custer was killed, along with two of his brothers, a
nephew, and a brother-in-law. The total American casualties,
including scouts, totaled 268 dead and 55 injured. Public response to
the Great Sioux War varied at the time. The battle, and Custer's
actions in particular, have been studied extensively by historians.

28) 1886 - Statue of Liberty is Dedicated

On October 28, 1886, France gave the US one of the most famous
symbols of Liberty in the Western World – the Statue of Liberty. It

commemorates the signing of the United States Declaration of Independence, and was given to the United States by the people of France to represent the friendship between the two countries established during the American Revolution. It represents a woman wearing a stola, a crown, and sandals; trampling a broken chain; raising a torch in her right hand; and holding a tabula ansata, where the date of the Declaration of Independence (JULY IV MDCCLXXVI) is written, in her left hand. The statue welcomes visitors, immigrants, and returning Americans traveling by ship.

The Statue of Liberty

The statue is made of a covering of pure copper, left to weather to a natural blue-green patina. Its framework is entirely made of steel, with the exception of the flame of the torch, which is coated in gold leaf. The statue sits on a rectangular stonework pedestal with a foundation in the shape of an irregular eleven-pointed star. The statue is 151 ft. (46 m) tall, but with the pedestal and foundation, it is 305 ft. (93 m) tall.

29) 1896 - Plessy v. Ferguson Decision Holds That Racial Segregation is Constitutional

The United States Supreme Court decision on May 18, 1896, regarding the case *Plessy v. Ferguson* was one of the most consequential court decisions in US history. It ruled that segregation was legal as long as equal facilities were provided for both races. The decision was handed down by a vote of 7 to 1.

An old picture of a restaurant in Lancaster, Ohio

Leading up to the decision, the State of Louisiana passed a law saying that whites and blacks had to ride in different cars on trains, but required that the trains be "equal." Homer Plessy, who was one-eighth black (meaning that one of his eight great-grandparents was black) was arrested for riding on a whites-only car. He challenged the Louisiana law, saying it was against the United States Constitution. Plessy argued that the state law that required East Louisiana Railroad to segregate trains had denied him his rights under the Thirteenth and Fourteenth Amendments to the United States Constitution. The Supreme Court then ruled that the Louisiana law was valid. It stated that requiring whites and blacks to ride in separate trains did not harm blacks in any way. In 1954, *Brown v. Board of Education* overturned the *Plessy v. Ferguson* ruling.

30) 1898 - USS *Maine* is Blown Up in Havana Harbor. US Declares War on Spain (Spanish–American War)

After the mysterious sinking of the US Navy battleship *Maine* in Havana Harbor, political pressures from the Democratic Party and certain industrialists pushed the administration of Republican President William McKinley into a war he had wished to avoid. On April 25, Congress declared war on Spain (after Spain had declared war on the US one day earlier). Volunteers throughout the country signed up for the war. Future president Theodore Roosevelt raised troops and became famous in leading the Rough Riders during the Battle of San Juan Hill.

The famous *Battle of Manila Bay*

The Spanish–American War was a short and one-sided war. Spain lost and had to give up its colonies of Cuba, the Philippines, Puerto Rico, and part of Guam. All of these colonies, except for Cuba, would later become US colonies. During the war, almost 400 American soldiers died during fighting, but more than 4,000 Americans died from diseases such as yellow fever, typhoid, and malaria.

31) 1917 - United States Enters World War I

The United States' entry into the first World War came in April 1917 after more than two years of efforts by President Woodrow Wilson to keep the country neutral during the conflict. Many Americans were clueless about the imminent war in Europe in the summer of 1914, and thousands of tourists were caught by surprise. The American government, under the Wilson administration, called for neutrality "in thought and deed." American public opinion went along with neutrality at first, especially among German Americans, Irish Americans and Swedish Americans, as well as among women and church leaders.

President Wilson before Congress, announcing the break in official relations with Germany on February 3, 1917.

However, the citizenry increasingly came to see the German Empire as the villain after news of atrocities in Belgium in 1914 and the sinking of the passenger liner RMS *Lusitania* in 1915 in defiance of international law. During the first months of 1917, Germany decided to resume all-out submarine warfare on every commercial ship headed toward England, realizing that this decision would almost certainly mean war with the United States. Publication of the Zimmermann Telegram (military alliance to Mexico) outraged Americans just as German U-boats (submarines) began sinking American ships in the North Atlantic. President Wilson asked Congress for "a war to end all wars" which would "make the world safe for democracy," and Congress voted to declare war on Germany on April 6, 1917. War on the Austro-Hungarian Empire was subsequently declared on December 7, 1917.

32) 1919 - Eighteenth Amendment Prohibits Alcohol

The Eighteenth Amendment to the United States constitution was ratified by January 16, 1919, and declared the production, transport, and sale of alcohol illegal (though not the consumption or private possession). It came into effect on January 16, 1920, and with it began the "Prohibition Era." Police would arrest anyone who was found making or selling alcohol illegally. The prohibition was mostly agitated by the Women's Christian Temperance Union and other reformist organizations.

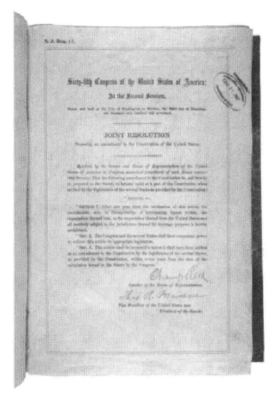

Picture of the 18th Amendment in the National Archives

Though its intentions were to establish a better society, the negative effects of the prohibition far outweighed its benefits. The police, courts, and prisons were overwhelmed with new cases; organized crime increased in power; and corruption extended among law enforcement officials. The amendment was repealed in 1933 by ratification of the Twenty-first Amendment, the only instance in United States history where a constitutional amendment was repealed in its entirety.

Today, states can regulate the selling of liquor by themselves.

33) 1923 - Teapot Dome Scandal Breaks

In the early 20th century, the US Navy started using oil fuel instead of coal. To ensure the Navy would always have enough fuel available, several oil-producing areas were designated as Naval Oil Reserves by President Taft. In 1922, Albert Fall leased the oil production rights at Teapot Dome to Mammoth Oil. He also leased the Elk Hills reserve to Pan American Petroleum. Both leases were issued without competitive bidding, but this practice was legal at that time.

Teapot Rock viewed from the south. The Teapot Dome oil fields are located north of the rock to the right.

What started the later-named "Teapot Dome Scandal" (the name of the oil field in Wyoming) was the money Fall received from the oil companies to change the terms of the lease in their favor. He received gifts totaling about $404,000 (about $5.34 million today). Fall attempted to keep his actions secret, but the sudden improvement in his standard of living was suspect. Prior to

Watergate, this was considered "greatest and most sensational scandal in the history of American politics."

34) 1927 - Charles Lindbergh Makes First Solo Nonstop Transatlantic Flight

Charles Lindbergh became one of the most famous men in the first half of the 20th century when he managed to be the first person to fly solo (alone) and non-stop across the Atlantic Ocean. His trip took him 33.5 hours (May 20-21) from Roosevelt Airfield in New York to Paris, flying in his single-engine airplane, *The Spirit of St. Louis*.

The Spirit of St. Louis on display at the Smithsonian Museum in Washington D.C.

When Lindbergh arrived back in the United States, several warships and aircrafts escorted him to Washington, D.C., where President Calvin Coolidge awarded him the Distinguished Flying Cross. Lindbergh's act also won him the Orteig Prize, which included 25,000 U.S. dollars. One month later, a parade was held for him on 5th Avenue in New York City and at the end of 1927, he was named Time's first Man of the Year. After his flying career, Lindbergh served on several national and international committees and boards, including the central committee of the National Advisory Committee for Aeronautics in the United States.

35) 1929 - Stock Market Crash Precipitates Great Depression

The Wall Street Crash of 1929, also known as Black Tuesday, began in late October 1929 and was the most devastating stock market crash in the history of the United States, when taking into consideration the full extent and duration of its fallout. The crash followed a speculative boom that had taken hold in the late 1920s and signaled the beginning of the 10-year Great Depression that affected all Western industrialized countries.

An impoverished American family living in a shanty, around 1936

It had devastating effects in countries rich and poor. Personal income, tax revenue, profits, and prices dropped, while international trade plunged by more than 50%. Unemployment in the US rose to 25%, and in some countries rose as high as 33%. After the experience of the 1929 crash, stock markets around the world instituted measures to suspend trading in the event of rapid declines, claiming that the measures would prevent such panic sales.

James Weber

Becoming a World Power: From World War II to the Civil Rights Act

36) 1933 - New Deal Recovery Measures Are Enacted by Congress

The New Deal was a series of programs launched by President Franklin D. Roosevelt between 1933 and 1938. It was intended to solve the problems caused by the Great Depression (mainly unemployment and agricultural overproduction) and focused on what historians call the Three Rs: Relief, Recovery, and Reform. That is Relief for the unemployed and poor, Recovery of the economy to normal levels, and Reform of the financial system to prevent a repeat depression.

The WPA hired unemployed teachers to provide free adult education programs.

Many historians distinguish between a "First New Deal" (1933–34) and a "Second New Deal" (1935–38), with the second one more liberal and more controversial. The "First New Deal" (1933–34) dealt with the pressing banking crises through the Emergency Banking Act and the 1933 Banking Act, which provided $500 million for relief operations by states and cities. The "Second New Deal" in 1935–38 included the controversial Works Progress Administration relief program, which instantly made the federal government by far the largest single employer in the nation, and the Social Security Act. By 1936, the term "liberal" was typically used for supporters of the New Deal, and "conservative" for its opponents.

37) 1941 - The United States Enters World War II

During the first two years of the global conflict, the United States had maintained formal neutrality while supplying Britain, the Soviet Union, and China with war material through the Lend-Lease Act, which was signed into law on March 11, 1941, as well as deploying the US military to replace the British invasion forces in Iceland. After the surprise attack by the Japanese and sinking of the main battleship fleet at Pearl Harbor, the US officially entered the war on December 11, 1941.

USS *Arizona* during the Japanese surprise air attack on the
American pacific fleet, December 7, 1941

During the war, over 16 million Americans served in the United
States Armed Forces, with 290,000 killed in action and 670,000
wounded. There were also 130,201 American POWs, of whom
116,129 returned home after the war. Key civilian advisors to
President Franklin D. Roosevelt included Secretary of War Henry
Stimson, who mobilized the nation's industries and induction centers
to supply the Army, commanded by General George C. Marshall, and
the Army Air Forces under General Hap Arnold. The war in Europe
ended with an invasion of Germany by the Western Allies and the
Soviet Union, culminating in the capture of Berlin by Soviet and
Polish troops and the subsequent German unconditional surrender
on May 8, 1945.

Following the Potsdam Declaration by the Allies on July 26, 1945, the United States dropped atomic bombs on the Japanese cities of Hiroshima and Nagasaki on August 6 and August 9, respectively. With an invasion of the Japanese archipelago imminent, the possibility of additional atomic bombings, and the Soviet Union's declaration of war on Japan and invasion of Manchuria, Japan surrendered on August 15, 1945. Thus ended the war in Asia and the final destruction of the Axis bloc.

38) 1948 - Marshall Plan and Berlin Blockade

After World War II ended, many parts of Europe were destroyed and needed to be rebuilt quickly. US officials therefore implemented the Marshall Plan (officially called the European Recovery Program [ERP]), which gave $13 billion (approximately $160 billion in current dollar value) in economic support to help rebuild European economies and stop communism. The plan ran for four years beginning in April 1948. The goals of the United States were to rebuild war-devastated regions, remove trade barriers, modernize industry, and make Europe prosperous again. The project is seen as successful because by the time it ended, the economy of every member state had grown well past pre-war levels.

Airplanes unloading at Tempelhof Airport during the Berlin
Airlift.

That same year, one of the first major international crises of the Cold
War took place. After the occupation of post–World War II
Germany, the Soviet Union blocked the Western Allies' railway, road,
and canal access to the sectors of Berlin under Allied control. This
was in response to the recent monetary reform in the three German
Occupation zones controlled by the Western powers, which the
Soviet Union feared made West Germany too strong. The Soviets
offered to drop the blockade if the Western Allies withdrew the
newly introduced Deutschmark from West Berlin. The Western
Allies then organized the Berlin airlift to carry supplies to the people
in West Berlin. Aircrews from the United States Air Force, the British
Royal Air Force, the Royal Canadian Air Force, the Royal Australian
Air Force, the Royal New Zealand Air Force, and the South African
Air Force flew over 200,000 flights in one year, providing up to 8,893

tons of necessities, such as fuel and food, to the Berliners daily. By the spring of 1949, the airlift was clearly succeeding, and by April, it was delivering more cargo than had previously been transported into the city by rail. On May 12, 1949, the USSR lifted the blockade of West Berlin.

39) 1950 - Beginning of the Korean War

The Korean War arose from the division of Korea at the end of World War II and from the global tensions of the Cold War that developed immediately afterwards. By 1948, two separate governments had been set up – one in the north by the Soviets and one in the south by the United States. Both governments claimed to be the legitimate government of Korea, and neither side accepted the border as permanent. The conflict escalated into open warfare when North Korean forces invaded South Korea on June 25, 1950.

Combat in the streets of Seoul

The North, led by communist Kim Il-Sung, was supported mostly by the People's Republic of China and the USSR. The South, led by nationalist Syngman Rhee, received help from the United Nations, and especially from the United States. After three years of fighting and more than two million Koreans dead, the war ended in a truce, though even today, South Korea and North Korea are still officially at war, and the United States still keeps troops in South Korea. North and South Korea are now divided by the 38th parallel, with the border heavily guarded day and night.

40) 1951 - Twenty-Second Amendment Limits Presidency to Two Terms

The Twenty-second Amendment to the United States Constitution limits any presidency to two terms, or eight years. Before the ratification of the Twenty-second Amendment, the Constitution had no limit on how many times a person could be elected as president. The nation's first president, George Washington, chose not to try to be elected for a third term. This suggests that two terms were enough for any president, and Washington's two-term limit became the unwritten rule for all Presidents until 1940.

1944 campaign poster for Roosevelt's fourth term.

This changed with Franklin Delano Roosevelt when he won a third term in 1940 and a fourth in 1944. Roosevelt was a popular president who had brought the US through the Great Depression of the 1930s and almost all of World War II. He died in April 1945, just months after the start of his fourth term. Near the end of the 1944 campaign, Republican nominee Thomas E. Dewey, the governor of New York, announced support of an amendment that would limit future presidents to two terms. According to Dewey, "Four terms, or sixteen years, is the most dangerous threat to our freedom ever proposed." Soon after, the Republican-controlled Congress approved the 22nd Amendment in March 1947, and nearly four years later, in February 1951, enough states ratified the amendment for its adoption.

41) 1955 - Vietnam War

The Vietnam War was the second proxy war fought in Asia, and was part of the Cold War. It lasted from 1955 to 1975 and was officially fought between North Vietnam and South Vietnam, but both sides were heavily supported by either communist or Western countries. North Vietnam was supported by the USSR, China, and North Korea, while South Vietnam was supported by the United States with its allies: Thailand, Australia, New Zealand, and the Philippines.

A US tank convoy in Vietnam

The US government viewed American involvement in the war as a way to prevent a Communist takeover of South Vietnam. This was part of a wider containment strategy with the stated aim of stopping the spread of communism. According to the US domino theory, if one state went Communist, other states in the region would follow, and US policy thus held that Communist rule over all of Vietnam was unacceptable. The North Vietnamese government and the Viet Cong were fighting to reunify Vietnam under communist rule. They used guerrilla tactics, which included booby traps and underground caves, to make up for the lack of fighting power.

42) 1959 - Alaska and Hawaii Become Official States

In 1959, the United States admitted two new states to the nation. First, on January 3, came Alaska. The United States bought Alaska from Russia in 1867 (see the Alaska Purchase). Later that year (August 21), the island group of Hawaii was also admitted. The first people of Hawaii were Polynesians, who came to the islands sometime between 200 and 600 AD. Captain James Cook is given credit for discovering the islands for the Europeans in 1778. In January 1893, Queen Lili'uokalani was overthrown and replaced by a provisional government composed of members of the American Committee of Safety. American lawyer Sanford B. Dole became President of the Republic when the Provisional Government of Hawaii ended on July 4, 1894.

1897 cartoon: Uncle Sam lays a claim to Hawaii and warns off
Japan, Britain, and France

Congress passed the Hawaii Admission Act in March 1959 and US
President Dwight D. Eisenhower signed it into law. The act excluded
Palmyra Atoll, which had been part of the Kingdom and Territory of
Hawaii, from statehood. On June 27 of that year, a referendum asked
residents of Hawaii to vote on the statehood bill. The Hawaii
electorate voted 94.3% "yes for statehood" to 5.7% "no." The
choices were to accept the Act or to remain a territory, without the
option of independence. The act made Hawaii the fiftieth American
state.

43) 1964 - Civil Rights Act is Signed

President Lyndon B. Johnson signed the Civil Rights Act into law on July 2, 1964. It was a landmark piece of civil rights legislation that outlawed discrimination based on race, color, religion, sex, or national origin, and was the result of the Civil Rights Movement led by Martin Luther King, Jr., who had delivered his "I Have a Dream" speech one year earlier.

Lyndon B. Johnson signs the Civil Rights Act of 1964. Among the guests is Martin Luther King, Jr.

The Civil Rights Act outlawed unequal application of voter registration requirements and racial segregation in schools, at the workplace, and by facilities that served the general public. Powers given to enforce the act were initially weak, but were supplemented during later years. Congress asserted its authority to legislate under several different parts of the United States Constitution, principally its power to regulate interstate commerce under Article One, its duty to guarantee all citizens equal protection of the laws under the Fourteenth Amendment, and its duty to protect voting rights under the Fifteenth Amendment.

44) 1969 - Apollo 11 Lands on the Moon

Launched by a Saturn V rocket from Kennedy Space Center in Florida, on July 16, 1969, Apollo 11 was the fifth manned mission of NASA's Apollo program. The Apollo spacecraft had three parts: a Command Module (CM) with a cabin for the three astronauts, and the only part that landed back on Earth; a Service Module (SM), which supported the Command Module with propulsion, electrical power, oxygen, and water; and a Lunar Module (LM) for landing on the   Moon.

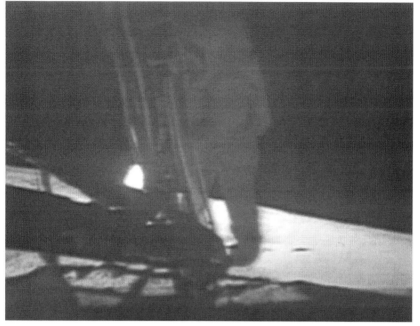

Neil Armstrong descends a ladder to become the first human to step onto the surface of the Moon.

After being sent toward the Moon by the Saturn V's upper stage, the astronauts separated the spacecraft from it and traveled for three days until they entered into lunar orbit. Armstrong and Aldrin then moved into the Lunar Module and landed in the Sea of Tranquility. They stayed a total of about 21½ hours on the lunar surface. After lifting off in the upper part of the Lunar Module and rejoining Collins in the Command Module, they returned to Earth and landed in the Pacific Ocean on July 24.

James Weber

A Modern America: From
Apollo 11 to Hurricane Katrina

45) 1972 - Watergate Affair breaks

Watergate is probably the most famous political scandal in the 20th century. It broke out because of the June 17, 1972, break-in of the Democratic National Committee (DNC) headquarters at the Watergate office complex in Washington, D.C., and the Nixon administration's attempted cover-up of its involvement. When the conspiracy was discovered and investigated by the US Congress, the Nixon administration's resistance to its probes led to a constitutional crisis.

The Watergate Complex

The illegal activities included bugging the offices of political opponents and people of whom Nixon or his officials were suspicious and harassment of activist groups using FBI, the CIA, and the IRS. The scandal led to the discovery of multiple abuses of power by the Nixon administration, articles of impeachment, and the resignation of Richard Nixon in 1974—the only resignation of a US President to date. The scandal also resulted in the indictment of 69 people, with trials or pleas resulting in 48 being found guilty and incarcerated, many of whom were Nixon's top administration officials.

46) 1983 - Invasion of Granada

The Invasion of Grenada, ordered by President Ronald Reagan and codenamed Operation Urgent Fury, was an invasion of the nation of Grenada. Grenada is an island in the Caribbean Sea, 100 miles north of Venezuela, and more than 1,500 miles southeast of the United States. It gained independence from the United Kingdom in 1974 but retained the British monarch as head of state. The leftist New Jewel Movement, which was seen favorably by much of the Grenadan population, seized power in a coup in 1979, suspending the constitution. The 1983 invasion was triggered by the house arrest and murder of the leader of the coup that had brought a revolutionary government to power for the preceding four years.

Black Hawk helicopters over Granada

Grenada was invaded by the combined strength of troops from the United States (about 10,000 troops), Jamaica, and members of the Regional Security System, which resulted in a US victory within a matter of weeks. The military government was deposed and replaced by a government appointed by Governor-General Paul Scoon until elections were held in 1984. While the invasion enjoyed broad public support in the United States, it was criticized by the United Kingdom and Canada. An attempted United Nations General Assembly resolution, which would have condemned it as "a flagrant violation of international law," was vetoed by the United States in the Security Council.

47) 1991 - (Persian) Gulf War

In 1990, Iraq accused Kuwait of stealing Iraqi petroleum through slant drilling, and the conflict eventually led to the invasion of Kuwait under Iraqi dictator Saddam Hussein. Some feel there were several reasons for the Iraqi move, including Iraq's inability to pay more than US $80 billion that had been borrowed to finance the Iran–Iraq war, and Kuwaiti overproduction of petroleum, which kept revenues down for Iraq. The invasion started on August 2, 1990, and within two days of intense combat, most of the Kuwaiti Armed Forces were either overrun by the Iraqi Republican Guard or escaped to neighboring Saudi Arabia and Bahrain.

Persian Gulf Veterans National Medal of the US military

The Iraqi Army's occupation of Kuwait was met with international condemnation, and brought immediate economic sanctions against Iraq by members of the U.N. Security Council. US President George H. W. Bush deployed US forces into Saudi Arabia and urged other countries to send their own forces to the scene. After no agreement between Iraq and the U.N. could be reached, the US began an aerial and naval bombardment on January 17, 1991, continuing for five weeks. This was followed by a ground assault in February, which marked a decisive victory for the Coalition forces, who drove the Iraqi military from Kuwait and advanced into Iraqi territory. Even though the military operations in Iraq is seen as a success from an American point of view, it led to further conflicts in the region (e.g. Iraq War 2003).

48) 2001 - 9/11 Attacks on World Trade Center

The September 11, 2001 attacks marked a series of four coordinated terrorist attacks launched by the Islamic terrorist group al-Qaeda on the United States in New York City and Washington, D.C. Four groups of terrorists, each with a trained pilot, captured airplanes and flew them into US landmarks, including the World Trade Center's twin towers in New York City and the Pentagon. A fourth plane crashed in an empty field in Pennsylvania before reaching its target in Washington, D.C. During the terrorist attacks, nearly 3000 people died.

Remains of the South Tower after the suicide attacks

Suspicion quickly fell on al-Qaeda. Although the group's leader, Osama bin Laden, initially denied any involvement, he claimed responsibility for 9/11 in 2004. As reason for the attacks, Al-Qaeda and bin Laden cited the presence of American troops in Saudi Arabia, US support of Israel and sanctions against Iraq as motives. The United States responded by launching the War on Terror and invading Afghanistan to depose the Taliban, which had harbored al-Qaeda. Many countries strengthened their anti-terrorism legislation and expanded law enforcement powers. Having evaded capture for almost ten years, bin Laden was located and killed by US forces in May 2011.

49) 2003 - Iraq War

The US invaded Iraq on March 20, 2003. It was joined by the United Kingdom, as well as several coalition allies, and launched a shock and awe surprise attack without a former declaration of war. Iraqi forces were quickly overwhelmed as US troops swept through the country. The Bush Administration based its rationale for war principally on the assertion that Iraq possessed weapons of mass destruction (WMDs) and that Saddam's government posed an immediate threat to the United States and its coalition allies.

US tanks at the Hands of Victory monument in Baghdad

The invasion led to the collapse of the dictatorship and the capture of Saddam Hussein in December 2003, who was executed by a military court in 2006. Unfortunately, the power vacuum following Saddam's demise along with mismanagement of the occupation led to widespread sectarian violence between Sunnis and Shias, as well as a lengthy insurgency against American and coalition forces. The US started withdrawing its troops in the winter of 2007–2008 and the winding down of US involvement in the country accelerated under President Barack Obama. The US formally withdrew all combat troops from Iraq by December 2011.

50) 2005 - Hurricane Katrina

Hurricane Katrina was one of the most devastating natural disasters, as well as one of the deadliest hurricanes, in the history of the United States. The storm formed over the Bahamas on August 23, 2005, where it moved east and hit Florida as a Category 1 hurricane two days later. Katrina then crossed over Florida and strengthened into a Category 5 hurricane in the Gulf of Mexico. The storm then hit Louisiana and Mississippi on the morning of August 29. The leftovers of Katrina then died out over the Great Lakes on August 31.

Flooded New Orleans and Metairie, Louisiana

The damages Katrina brought were so bad that 80% of New Orleans was flooded when the levees to the city broke. Most of the people killed by Katrina were thought to have died from drowning. Due to the catastrophic emergency management by the city and the National

Guard, many government officials were criticized for their responses, including New Orleans Mayor Ray Nagin, Louisiana Governor Kathleen Blanco, and President George W. Bush.

If you enjoyed this book, please consider leaving a review on Amazon. Reviews help us authors out a lot and I would love to know what you thought about my work.

Sincerely
James Weber

James Weber

Other Books in the *History in 50 Events* Series

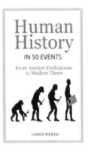  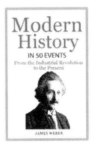 

  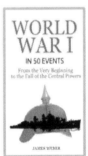 

Made in the USA
Middletown, DE
29 November 2016